play the music of
Burt Bacharach

Music Minus One

3974

SUGGESTIONS FOR USING THIS MMO EDITION

WE HAVE TRIED to create a product that will provide you an easy way to learn and perform these compositions with a full ensemble in the comfort of your own home. The following MMO features and techniques will help you maximize the effectiveness of the MMO practice and performance system:

Because it involves a fixed accompaniment performance, there is an inherent lack of flexibility in tempo. We have observed generally accepted tempi, and always in the originally intended key, but some may wish to perform at a different tempo, or to slow down or speed up the accompaniment for practice purposes; or to alter the piece to a more comfortable key. You can purchase from MMO specialized CD players & recorders which allow variable speed while maintaining proper pitch, and vice versa. This is an indispensable tool for the serious musician and you may wish to look into purchasing this useful piece of equipment for full enjoyment of all your MMO editions.

We want to provide you with the most useful practice and performance accompaniments possible. If you have any suggestions for improving the MMO system, please feel free to contact us. You can reach us by e-mail at *info@musicminusone.com*.

Music Minus One

3974

contents

COMPLETE VERSION TRACK	MINUS VERSION TRACK		PAGE
	11	Tuning	
1	12	I Say a Little Prayer	4
2	13	Blue on Blue	6
3	14	Alfie	8
4	15	Wives and Lovers (Hey, Little Girl)	10
5	16	Walk on By	12
6	17	Magic Moments	14
7	18	Windows of the World	16
8	19	Do You Know the Way to San Jose	18
9	20	This Guy's in Love with You	20
10	21	What the World Needs Now Is Love	22

I SAY A LITTLE PRAYER

Words by Hal David
Music by Burt Bacharach
Arranged by Jack Six

BLUE ON BLUE

Lyric by Hal David
Music by Burt Bacharach
Arranged by Jack Six

ALFIE
Theme from the Paramount Picture ALFIE

Words by Hal David
Music by Burt Bacharach
Arranged by Jack Six

sure as I be-lieve there's a heav-en a-bove, "Al-fie?" I

know there's some-thing much more. Some-thing e-ven non-be-liev-ers

can be-lieve in. I be-lieve in love, "Al-fie?"

With-out true love we just ex-ist, "Al-fie?" Un-til you find the love you've

missed you're noth-ing, "Al-fie?" When you walk let your heart

lead the way and you'll find love an-y day, "Al-fie,"

"Al - fie."

WIVES AND LOVERS
(Hey, Little Girl)
from the Paramount Picture WIVES AND LOVERS

Words by Hal David
Music by Burt Bacharach
Arranged by Jack Six

wives should al-ways be lov-ers too. Run to his arms the mo-ment he comes home to

you. He's al - most here. Hey, lit-tle girl, bet-ter wear some-thing

pret - ty, some - thing you'd wear to go to the cit - y; and dim all the

lights, pour the wine, start the mus - ic, time to get read - y for love.

(Sax-ad lib.) (Strgs.)

(81-88) (89-96)

Solo

Hey, lit-tle girl, bet-ter wear some-think pret-ty, some - thing you'd

wear to go to the cit - y; and dim all the lights, pour the wine, start the

mus - ic, time to get read - y for love. Oh, time to get read - y,

time to get read - y, time to get read - y for love.

pizz.

WALK ON BY

Lyric by Hal David
Music by Burt Bacharach
Arranged by Jack Six

If you see me walk-in' down the street and I start to cry each time we meet,
I just can't get o-ver los-in' you and so if I seem bro-ken and blue,

walk on by, walk on by.

Make be - lieve that you don't see the tears, just let me grieve in
Fool - ish pride, that's all that I have left. So let me hide the

pri - vate 'cause each time I see you, I break down and cry.
tears and the sad - ness you gave me when you said good - bye.

Walk on by, walk on by, walk on by.

MAGIC MOMENTS

Lyric by Hal David
Music by Burt Bacharach
Arranged by Jack Six

MMO 3974

The tel - e - phone call that tied up the line for hours and hours,
The pen - ny ar - cade, the games that we played, the fun and the priz - es,

The sat - ur - day Dance you got up the nerve to send you some flow - ers;
The hal - low - een hop when ev - 'ry - one came in fun - ny dis - guis - es;

Mag - ic mo - ments, mem - 'ries we've been shar - ing.

Mag - ic mo - ments, when two hearts are car - ing.

Time can't e - rase the mem - - - 'ry of these

mag - ic mo - ments filled with love.

filled with love.

(Orch.)   Rall.- - - - - - - - - -

THE WINDOWS OF THE WORLD

Lyric by Hal David
Music by Burt Bacharach
Arranged by Jack Six

DO YOU KNOW THE WAY TO SAN JOSE

Lyric by Hal David
Music by Burt Bacharach
Arranged by Jack Six

THIS GUY'S IN LOVE WITH YOU

Words by Hal David
Music by Burt Bacharach
Arranged by Jack Six

WHAT THE WORLD NEEDS NOW IS LOVE

Words by Hal David
Music by Burt Bacharach
Arranged by Jack Six

Engraving: Wieslaw Novak

MMO 3974

MUSIC MINUS ONE
50 Executive Boulevard
Elmsford, New York 10523-1325
800-669-7464 (U.S.)/914-592-1188 (International)

www.musicminusone.com
e-mail: info@musicminusone.com